# OF WHEAT A

## Thoughts on the Nature a

Christopher Houghton Budd

*Dedicated to all who strive for a truly human economic life*

First published 1988 by
New Economy Publications
Canterbury, Kent, England

Reprinted (revised) 1996



British Library Catalogue-in-Print Data
A CIP catalogue record for this book
is available from the British Library

ISBN 0 948229 01 2

Printed by Booksprint
Bristol, England

# CONTENTS

# INTRODUCTION

Written across the worried face of modern humanity is the simple, stark question:- What is money? Various schools of thought exist offering several definitions of money, and a variety of experiments have been and continue to be made with money in the practical sphere. But how in reality can money be more than one thing? Its forms, functions and applications may vary, but surely in essence it has to be one thing. One thing, capable of many expressions. That, at any rate, is the proposition of this essay. I hope to show that a single concept of money is able to explain all the many phenomena connected with it. In the process I propose to describe how money needs to be treated today if it is to conform to humanity's strivings for peace and freedom.

Insufficient attention is paid to the fact that peace and freedom in our time are everywhere undermined, thwarted, contradicted and attacked by the inappropriate form of money with which we conduct our lives today. Modify money, and many of the world's social ills will admit to remedies. Persist with the kind of money now in use, and the world's inequities can only increase and become compounded. Today's revolution in the field of computers provides the essential technological means to effect change in the world's money. We have now only to understand and carry out the necessary modifications. Refuse, and the automated, electronic money of computer termini will weigh even more heavily on the human soul than it does today. That which has the potential to further liberate the human being, can, if developed without a parallel increase in human consciousness, also work in the other direction - enslaving those who would be free.

# 1: MONEY

## MONEY IN ITS OWN RIGHT

Definitions of money vary, depending on the time and place in economic history of their authors. People refer to money as "a store of value", as a "medium of exchange", and so on. Because of its nature, money fulfils many functions and each definition has a degree of validity, provided one understands it to be a definition of a particular function of money, rather than of money as such, of money from a particular point of view rather than in its totality. Taken all together, the various definitions of money might add up to a single definition, but it would be wiser and more informative to dispense with the word "definition" in this context and to think more in terms of "description". To *describe* money leads one to a deeper and more comprehensive picture of it than attempts to define it ever can. Indeed, therein lies a major methodological clue as regards economic science. Something as connected to life as money defies being put into a neat box, but it reveals its secrets when it is followed in its course through life.

For the purposes of this essay, I would prefer to set forth the understanding of money on which the rest of this text will rely, leaving for another occasion a debate as to the "correctness" of this view over against those held by other schools of economic thought.

Economic life takes place on the basis of trade - a ceaseless process of transactions whereby men exchange the values they have created for those they need and will use up. Additionally, one can see that each party to a transaction enters into it also with a view to profiting from it. Something over and above a mere swap is sought by both parties, something without which there would be little incentive to trade. Whether it takes the form of our trying to sell as high as possible- or to buy as low as possible, the economic effect is the same - to profit from the exchange of values - to create a surplus.

Since both parties to a transaction are of one mind in this respect, it is an error to think that in an exchange the profit of one party is the loss of the other. In reality each party profits. The combined effect is not a profit on one side and a loss on the other, but a dual surplus. It is fundamental to understand this idea and never to lose sight of it. In the labyrinth of economics, this idea is the thread of Ariadne, without which one is lost. Moreover, within this idea lies another - that of the *process of exchange* accompanied by, or giving rise to, the *process of surplus* whereby surpluses are constantly generated over and above the mere exchange of values.

The gain in value to both parties is the true aim of every transaction, and because this process is emancipated from the mere swapping of barter, it is also the origin of money and the reason why not only goods circulate, but money too. Money is not merely a representative of goods and material values. It is something in its own right.

To say that money is something in its own right is not, however, to say that it is something unto itself. There is a point midway between being a part of a matrix and becoming a world unto oneself. The struggle is to find the right form of money, one that is neither tied to goods, nor that has gone off on its own, as it were. When money becomes something unto itself it acts like a cancer in economic life, creating a rival centre and consuming the economic life proper in just the same way as physical cancer disturbs and consumes the organism it occupies. It is this, unfortunately, that modern money has more or less become. Having freed itself from the material economy, it has now turned against that economy. As a result, whereas money tied to goods prevents humanity's healthy development, money opposed to goods undermines it. Healthy development (both economic and cultural) relies on a form of money that combines both poles instead of opposing the one to the other.

The crisis in the understanding of money is indicated by two modern phenomena - increasing abstraction in the form and manner of dealing with money on the one hand (computer figures, the "Big Bang", derivatives, etc), and the search by growing numbers of monetary reformers for a "real" money [see Appendix 1] on the other. While some would set the two developments apart and suggest that one should prevail over the other, in the opinion of this writer such an approach to life is rarely productive and little commends itself. In contrast, careful observation of *both* developments promises greater rewards in terms of insights. Indeed, the very duality that characterises most modern thinking about money provides a major clue to understanding its true nature.

Money is difficult to grasp - being at once concrete and abstract, representing both material wealth and ideas. It has forms that are more readily understood like coinage - but it also expresses itself intangibly, as in bank credits. Money, because of what it is, must be tangible at one place and intangible at another. It does not do to issue edicts saying that money should only be tangible, for example. The form money takes follows on the function it is fulfilling, arid since money fulfils various functions from buying goods to financing ideas - the need is to ensure that the forms it takes at any one place or time are true to its functions at that place or time.

For this, a fluid, not a fixed idea of money is necessary.

## MOVING BOOKKEEPING

Consider the idea that money is a form of moving bookkeeping. This thought cannot be understood with a fixed idea about money. On the contrary, it presupposes mobile concepts and as an idea is self eloquent - speaking directly of money as something in movement, something dynamic.

A thing in movement cannot be understood as something static. In philosophical terms, the issue is whether money is something unto itself o r representative of other things. We become Kantian when we think that money can be a thing in itself, independent of and divorced from the world around it. It is necessary to see through this; to see that money is only representative of other things. This does not mean that it cannot or does not on occasion come to rest, only that stasis is not its essential nature. The point is that a dynamic concept of money allows for fixed moments of money without suggesting it is inherently static. In contrast, static definitions of money allow no dynamism and force their differences into competition with one another. Only a dynamic economics, derived from mobile thinking, can synthesise them.

Consider three different things and three identical pieces of money of the same form - coins, say. Use one coin to buy some food. Use another to lend to your friend. And put the third in a charity box. Here the medium of the money (coinage) is constant, but the uses it is put to, the functions it serves are all different. The shopkeeper may in turn give the money he has received for the food to a charity; your friend may buy shoes; and the charity may give to someone in need. Money is a constant medium serving different functions.

When developed as an exercise, such an idea is a basic piece of dynamic economics. The purpose is to see the things that money represents, rather than the money as such. After all, today even physical money coinage - is metallurgically worthless. Its value derives from the number stamped on it, no longer from the substance of the coin itself.

Money today is at a remove from the real economy, comparable to the mercury in a thermometer. The thermometer and money are there to make understandable to us processes we are otherwise submerged within. By their means we can become aware of life's realities - but never can they replace these realities. Pushing the mercury down in a thermometer does not lower the temperature around it; reducing interest rates does not of itself increase the flow of money. (What it does is encourage people to divert the flow from savings into expenditure, for example but that is quite a different matter.)

## WEATHER, MONEY AND FLOW

The idea of money in movement is everywhere recognised, albeit unconsciously, by such words as "currency", "liquidity", "cash flow". We use the language of movement only partially awake to its significance.

The idea of flow, for example, is central. Consider the flow of the weather. The rain that falls from the sky once ran in our rivers and flowed in our seas, and will do so again. The cycle of water on the planet is the indispensable basis of all manner of processes, but the water is in constant flow. Even when water is made static - in a reservoir, for example - it is not static. Reserves are only delayed flows, held back until they are needed to flow again. Their meaning is not in themselves, but in their subsequent flowing.

Money is no different. Reserves of money are valuable only in terms of the future expenditure of them. They presuppose flow. Flow, not reserves, is primary.

Clearly, it is not possible to reserve all the water one needs; a reservoir is only a device for translating uncertain rainfall into constant supply. It is a temporary arrangement and rests in the end on the fact of repeated rainfall. Reservoirs translate into a constant process of flow what nature provides only intermittently.

The question is: Does one separate oneself off from or trust oneself to the overall process. The picture is clear. As is the choice. One relies on the overall process. Reservoirs only adapt life to human comfort. They cannot replace it. Value is maintained by circulation, not by isolation.
It is better to be the pipe, through which the water flows, albeit at different speeds, of course. The pipe constantly receives from one end and releases from the other. The direction of the flow may become reversed - but there is no other reality than that of flow as far as the idea of a pipe is concerned.

For human beings and money it is the same question: Do we experience and can we trust the flow of money? In the end, and in practice, we have no choice but to do so and, indeed, we do not do otherwise than receive money and pass it on. The miser who creates an enormous reservoir through his refusal to expend, only does so until his death. Even the reserves on a balance sheet are not to be found in a box under the bank's counter. They are out in the economy. The bank is entitled to them, but that is a different matter. It does not physically keep them, because under the mattress money loses its value - as anyone who has kept money in this way well knows.

Flow is the reality of economic life. The real value of money depends on its flow. Reserves are used to control flow, but they cannot and do not supplant it. In order to understand money in movement, therefore, it is essential to experience, recognise, trust and render tangible the inherent flow of money.

In more technical terms one speaks of the circulation of money, and of the speed of circulation. The slower the circulation the lower the value of the money. Decrease the speed of turnover in a shop and you decrease its profitability. This is an important picture and relationship. Below a certain speed of turnover a business cannot operate. Above that speed its profit increases proportionately, provided no undue increase in expenditure is necessitated.

| Ratio 10:8 | 1 | 2 | 3 | 4 | 5 | 6 |
|---|---|---|---|---|---|---|
| Turnover | 10,000 | 12,000 | 14,000 | 16,000 | 18,000 | 20,000 |
| Costs | 8,000 | 8,000 | 8,000 | 12,800 | 12,800 | 12,800 |
| Profit | 2,000 | 4,000 | 6,000 | 3,200 | 5,200 | 7,200 |

In this example the value of the business is increased by the speed of turnover. On a given cost basis (columns 1-3) the turnover rises and with it the profit. A point is reached when the turnover necessitates an increase in costs - for example, extra staff or new equipment. The profit then falls for a time until the turnover rises further (columns 4-6), and so on. In the same way money depends for its value on its speed of circulation. That is the dilemma before us:the value of money is reduced by saving, hoarding, possessing, reserving. It is increased (that is to say, kept constant) by being kept in movement, in circulation.

This is not to say that reserves have no place. It is only to indicate that their place is limited and specific, and that they can readily become uneconomic. They bring the danger of wanting to stop the world in order to get off, of not wanting to be in the boat when it sinks. But all such notions are foolish as regards the economic life for it is a totality which includes us all. No-one escapes! The more one understands circulation and flow, the less conscious one is of money as such, and the more aware of the things it represents.

One who studies a balance sheet has to do this. He has to picture to himself what the many figures represent. He does it by reference to liquidity and other ratios. But ratios are relationships, b y definition. They are not static. One has to go further to see, for example, whether the stated debtors are likely to pay; perhaps visiting them to see if they have leather on their shoes and smiles on their faces! In other words, one seeks out real factors. The figures in themselves are meaningless. They were different ten minutes before and have changed in the time it took to understand them. They are, moreover, after the fact.

By implication, therefore, the balance sheet - the financial position at a moment in time - has to be, and is, read in movement, in terms of time and, of equal importance, in terms of forces affecting the business from outside it.

The figures all represent different things - fixed assets, depreciation, debtors, creditors, loans, profits and losses, capital but they are all denominated in one currency. One observes in this that very many different things are expressed in the one medium.

Nowadays it is possible to use a computer to provide continuous and immediate updating of a business's finances. Were a programme devised that amended the balance sheet according to every transaction made, and if one were to observe the screen, one would see a picture not unlike the ceaseless change in photographed cloud and weather formations. Stop the film at a particular frame and one would experience the balance sheet for what it is; a moment in time, but a moment now gone. One would experience the balance sheet as an abstraction and that movement is the essential reality.

What would this be other than moving bookkeeping?

Imagine further that the business being accounted were worldwide and that the computer programme also took into account exchange rates. In effect the denomination of the figures would represent a world currency, while the money would be in the form of figures.

Now, we today are used to abstract figures when it comes to money - £100, $300. But remove the £ sign or the $ and one is left with mere figures - 100, 300. These convey nothing to us. We give figures significance perforce of our connection to our national currencies. (For example, there is no denomination shown on the chart on page 12, but you will have subconsciously supplied your own.) This is the last obstacle to our directly experiencing world economy and world money as such, rather than our national economies and national currencies.

But what is figure-money? It is accounting, pure and simple. We are already in the age of money as moving bookkeeping.

## MONEY AND VALUES

The basic principle of money management is to ensure that money represents the total values in the economy at any one time - no more and no less. This fact takes many expressions, the most well-known being that there should always be enough money to purchase the goods available for sale. This, however, is not an exhaustive formulation, because it refers specifically to that aspect of money that represents physical values - commodities for sale.

Values - the substance of economic life - are not physical things, however. The value of any physical thing changes - witness the value of an article in an auction. This fact is sufficient to show that the value of something is not intrinsic to its substance or existence but hovers about it, so to speak, and exists largely in the minds of men. Physical things represent values but they are not synonymous with them. If this distinction is not understood and upheld, one commits an error in thought that can only result in erroneous economics. On the other hand, maintain this distinction and it provides the key to clear and powerful sight into the nature and workings of the economy.

Money must be equivalent to the values in the economy at any one time. It must follow their lead expanding when they expand, contracting when they contract. In this sense, money, like the mercury in a thermometer, reflects the conditions around it, but it does not determine them. One cannot lower the temperature in a room by pushing the mercury back down the thermometer. Likewise, one ought not to try to affect the economy by artificial manipulations of money. I say ought not to - but the problem is that one can.

Money, unlike the mercury in a thermometer, *can* affect its environment. One can freeze or overheat the economy by manipulating the money supply downwards or upwards. This is not a new fact in life, but it has quite new dimensions today. What is new is that ordinary men and women everywhere today can and do have direct and profound effects on the economy through the agency of money. It behoves them, therefore, to become more awake to the nature and workings of money. They then stand to see that their worries about money are to a large extent born of ignorance. In other words, that consciousness itself is a force that directly affects economic life and with it the value of money and all that that entails.

## TANGIBLE AND INTANGIBLE VALUES

Money must be equivalent to the values in the economy, but these values include factors that are both tangible and intangible. Chairs have a value, of course. But so do ideas. It is a fundamental mistake - but one usually made - to equate economic values only with physical goods. When this is done the idea arises.that money must be equivalent only to the value of the physical goods available for sale. This idea lies behind the thinking of all those who suggest that money should be denominated in terms of basic commodities be these raw materials, energy or essential foodstuffs.

While it is possible to imagine a world in which money represents only the goods available for sale, this condition is unobtainable in real life and never has obtained. Men have observed the exchange of goods in "pre-scientific" economies, for example, and seen there only the physical exchange, which they call barter. They have not seen or understood that this physical exchange is incidental to unseen motives and objectives on the part of those involved, whereby each party to a transaction seeks to gain from it - to receive values in addition to those he needs for his physical life. These additional values he requires in order to finance his development as a human being - a subtle permanent process whereby he seeks to emancipate himself from the confines of physical existence. Barter is an illusion in that it is an incomplete observation. The mere swapping of goods without consequential progress in development for each party is a life impossibility.

In addition to the physical economy, therefore, one needs to conceive an invisible economy, comprising ideas, feelings of security, relationships - any factors which have immediate economic significance but defy physical expression. The economy as a whole must be understood to comprise both tangible and intangible factors, while money, accordingly, must represent both.

Of course, the money in the economy may, at any one time, represent differing relationships between the two kinds of value - it may be more tangible at one moment, less so at another. Ideation waxes and wanes no less than the production of physical goods does. The Renaissance saw a huge increase in the amount of intangible values in the economy. In contrast, the mass production techniques of the twentieth century generate huge increases in the tangible values, although mass production can also be said to be a very powerful idea. Ideas and their effects have as great a reality in economic life as physical goods and their production. It is a false economics that regards ideas as less real than material goods, or, worse still, as not real at all.

## THE ECONOMY AS A WHOLE

To be true to the economy the nature, form and denomination of money must be faithful to the polar nature of economic life. The problem with modern money - abstract as it has become - is that it expresses more powerfully than ever before in human history the reality of the invisible aspect of economic life, but because we are conceptually unequipped to understand this intangible realm, it does so in a chaotic way.

As humanity becomes more self-conscious, more individual and more emancipated from the earth and from his social context, so he gives rise to a growing increase in the size of the invisible economy. The effect is that far more can be done on the basis of far less physical effort. Labour is constantly saved and saved enormously by the processes of individuation so much so that the economic reality of today is that we could all probably get by on a 2 day week. So enormous are the surpluses generated by the simple fact of the evolution of individuality that we completely delude ourselves when we speak of an absence of money or of an insufficiency of goods today. These are problems of our own making. One does not need economic theory to see this. One need only calculate the amount of effort expended in producing things which are merely destroyed (armaments, rockets, planned obsolescence, etc) in order to experience how much could be made available to humanity if this wealth were deployed instead in things we used up creatively, rather than threw away in deeds of destruction.

Today, therefore the size of the invisible economy is far greater than that of the physical one, a fact that is actually reflected in money today, were we but aware of it. Today's money represents not only physical goods already available for sale, but goods currently in production (credit, as ordinarily understood) and goods yet to be produced (over-extended credit, in common parlance).

Few people speak quite in these terms, of course. Money is described much more complicatedly. Yet it can be quite simply understood. Money must at all times be covered by, that is to say, represent something real. When we wish to redeem it the bank must be able to return equivalent values to us. This is basic financial psychology that needs no further rehearsing. Sometimes the money is covered by physical goods actually held physically for the purpose. For example, a bank may hold gold to the value of 1,000,000 and issue money to this level and no more (a ratio of 1 :1). If everyone then turned up at the same time, their money would be fully covered that is, refundable.

In the last few hundred years, through the development of individual consciousness and as evidenced in the evolution of banking, it has been experienced that not everyone seeks reimbursement at the same time. Only 10% of people do. Because this relationship has been consistently observed in life, the convention has developed of a deposit-to-reserve ratio greater than 1:1. Say, 10:1. For every 1 unit held by the bank, 10 are issued. The cover in this case is 10% tangible and physical, 90% intangible the intangibility in this case being assessments as to the probability of reimbursement.

Many people see in this a form of evil and they suppose devilish intentions on the part of bankers. This is a risky path of thought, however. Hard evidence, never supposition, should be the basis of thinking in this matter. It is not an easy enterprise, and not one that should be embarked upon lightly. Maybe there are evil-intentioned people active behind the scenes. Maybe not. In the nature of things they are unlikely to allow their unmasking, however, and seeking them out is an investigative pursuit that is best kept apart from economics. It has demonstrated little success in identifying, let alone arraigning, trying and sentencing its supposed suspects. And its effect in economics tends to be one of confusing thought.

In more recent times, with the introduction of SDR's [see Appendix 2] and the claimed severance from gold, the world's financial system has created a further form of cover - credits advanced against future assets. A mortgage on the future in effect. Rescheduling debts is another, increasingly prevalent, expression of the same phenomenon. It indicates that money exists way in excess of the values we have created or are in process of creating to date, and so it takes a charge on tomorrow's productivity.

Again, for many this is proof positive of incarnate evil in the world's money system. But, again, it may be better to reserve judgment. The huge extent of credit in relation to physical goods may be telling us something, if only we could listen or see carefully enough.

It is typical of materialist thought that it understands the past more readily than the future. It is, however, characteristic of economic life that it is future-oriented and that the past is past. In economic life, to cry over spilt milk is to spill even more. Modern money may seem grossly over-inflated and off the rails from the point of view of past-oriented thinking. But this phenomenon may be no more than the reality of economic life forcing itself in upon our consciousness - demanding that we think from the future to the past, not the other way round.

True economic thinking must begin in the future and work down to the past, for that is the nature of economic life. It comes out of the future, never out of the past. One invests in the light of expected future gains. One sends children to school in the expectation that they will "become something".

To orient one's thinking to the future is another way of speaking of intangible factors - because, of course, the future is by its very nature intangible to all except the seers among us.

Today's money can be said, therefore, to be drawing our attention to the need to understand that the economy as a whole comprises both tangible and intangible factors. It may also be warning us not to overlook the latter, or mistake them for the former.

## EMANCIPATED MONEY

It is clear, of course, that, compared to 1:1 cover by physical goods, money with a cover of 10:1 or more is abstract and to a certain extent divorced from the real economy. And, indeed, there are plenty of Shenandoah and Blue Ridge phenomena in our times that indicate the tendency for modern money to develop a life of its own. There is a real danger in our times that money, which previously had to follow the state of the economy, now determines it. Whereas money was once nothing other than an equivalence of goods produced, it now can be arbitrarily created and production of physical goods has to be increased to catch up with or "make good" the supply. It is the reverse of conventional wisdom and wreaks havoc in the minds and lives of those involved in modern economic life - which is all of us.

One needs to separate the baby from the bath water, however. Obviously, a money divorced from economic life we we can best do without. But a money that ties us to the drudgery of merely feeding ourselves is no more welcome a prospect. The problem is one of emancipating money without creating an abstraction. One can characterise money in former times as being tied to physical existence the period in economic history when we fancy that most people had no time for anything but working in order to eat. There is a need to be emancipated from this condition, to be free of it. But with the process of emancipation comes the danger of becoming separated off. Money, like the human being, must become something in its own right, emancipated from the matrix of its origins. But money, also like the human being, errs when it then becomes something unto itself.

Modern money, with all its attendant problems, can be brought into order and made sense of if one can understand the need for its emancipation, and if one understands how, in theory and in practice, this can be brought about. The wild horses can then be reined in, their direction harmonised, and their pace slowed down and made less erratic. Moreover, we all stand to enjoy a more comfortable ride as a consequence!

Emancipated money recognises the polarity of the tangible and intangible values that comprise the economic process. It gives to each due weight and does not prefer one over the other. Emancipated money neither discounts intangible factors in a pretence to equate itself to only physical goods, nor does it take off in a flight of fancy, disparaging, and in the process devaluing, the physical economy. Emancipated money frees one from earthly travail, but it does not result in the rape of the earth. If bondage to a round of eating to work, working to eat is the sign of tied money, the rape of the earth and the ruin of forests and farmland is the sign of disconnected money.

The fact that emancipated money recognises and gives value to both aspects of economic life, affords one a major clue to its nature. It is able to represent both physical and non-physical values - goods and credit, altering its formulation according to that which it currently represents. It can and does pass into every region of economic life, taking on the colour and language of each particular region as it goes. Truly cosmopolitan, emancipated money finds its essence in circulation. Its nature is to circulate, and to do so freely throughout the economy, going where it is needed, so to speak, and always following the contours of the economy as it finds them.

It is absolutely essential to understand that money is at its truest when it is the expression of circulation, uniting in continual movement the two poles of tangible and intangible values. But, whereas in theory one is able to draw a distinction between tangible and intangible values, between values being created and values being used up - between, in general economic terms, production a n d consumption - in practical life the distinction is not to be found in any precise form. Everywhere everything represents both tangible and intangible values. They pass through one another, depending on what has gone into them, the use they are to be put to and the circumstances of their owners, vendors or prospective purchasers.

Nowhere in practical life can tangible values be found separate from intangible values. For this reason, emancipated money has a dual nature and, when denominated, will express this dual nature - the polarity between sound ground and abstract idea.

# 2: SOUL ECONOMICS

## MONEY AND CONSCIOUSNESS

Money is the central question of the economic life. Through it one can develop an inner consciousness of economic life. But for this it is necessary to have an understanding of the human soul and of how it is related to economic life.

To the degree that it rests on materialism, economics does not take the human soul into account. Yet the soul is the seat of our experiences of the economy and it is in the soul, too, that our ideas arise. By paying careful attention to these experiences and to the origin of our ideas one can arrive at a real, rather than a hypothetical economics.

The fundamental condition of the human soul - the condition it seeks constantly because it is its natural state - is that of balance, equilibrium. It is no accident or mere theory that all economic life and all economic thinking is, similarly, in pursuit of balance. In a very real sense, economics builds on and belongs to the reality of the human soul.

Not only ideas arise in the soul, however, there are also forces of will. It is the forces of will that actually create economic life, guided by ideas. The fact that many ideas today are unworkable, and that many deeds done are unthinkable, is testimony to the separation and disconnectedness of our thinking and willing today. To become conscious of the human soul is to realise that therein thinking and willing combine and from there alone can issue practicable ideas and imaginative action.

I am well aware that the world of mere economic interests contradicts the idea of a "soul economics", and that economic life is often anything but balanced and harmonised. But chaotic economic life is the result of ill will, of negative will forces and selfishness; whereas goodwill restores confidence. The expression is, indeed, part of balance sheet terminology. Goodwill is the content of an expansive, humanitarian soul, without which economic life can and does not function properly.

This idea of a "soul economics" has a consequence for methodology. The nature of the soul is to connect everything together, to create a whole out of life. To combine all one's experiences and ideas in an ongoing process, a constant synthesising of life that underlies one's every action. Soul economics is characterised by this holism. Materialistic economics, on the other hand, swamps the human being in abstraction and unconnected details. It surrounds our consciousness on all sides with figures, graphs, formulae and theoretical notions that lack meaning in themselves and fail to convey a sense of reality. We drink them in and repeat them without knowing the assumptions they are based on, or whether these assumptions are correct or not. In contrast, soul economics offers large imaginative pictures of the economic life, arriving at detail from a totality, so that the detail always has a context and one can see its connection to an overall picture.

## NATURE AND SPIRIT

One such picture is that of the human being standing between nature on the one side and spirit on the other, by which I mean the physical world from which we derive our food, and the world of ideas, from which we derive another sort of nutrition.

There is a saying: as above, so below. Applied to economics, this saying has the meaning that nature reflects the spirit. All economics is in error if this relationship is not understood or recognised. Materialism in particular would have us think that the spiritual worlds are mere emanations of the forces of production. But it is also possible to conceive the forces of production as the reflections on earth of spiritual realities. The point is that man stands between these two, between nature "beneath" him and spirit "above" him.

Economic life arises between these two poles but without preference for either. The economic process weaves through and around them in a lemniscatory fashion. Strictly speaking, economics is concerned with the production and consumption of values. This process results in the production and consumption of goods, on the side of nature, and the creation of and application of capacities, on the side of spirit.

Nature and spirit are like two pillars at either side of the entrance to economic life. Neither can be dispensed with; neither is predominant. The key is the human being who necessarily stands between the two and must realise the relationship between them.

Spirit and nature are "givens". They precede the economic life as such. Economically they exist potentially as the basis but not the content of economic life. In the same way that education develops the capacities of an individual but does not create them and that a seed in the earth is transformed by the forces of nature, but does not create these forces.

By the word "spirit" I mean all the capacities inherent in the individual. By "nature" I mean all the processes of nature - the cycle of the seasons, growth and decay, the circulation of air, and so on.

If one thinks of the rivers, the sun, nuclear forces, of growth and decay - one thinks of aspects of nature that one cannot see physically. One can see their effects, but the forces themselves are invisible. They are behind the phenomena. In this sense one can form a picture of nature. If one thinks of the weather, of the movement of the earth, of the existence of the sun one thinks of nature. Of a higher order than the outer phenomena themselves is the fact that there is weather, that there is movement of the earth, that the sun exists. To deepen one's understanding of nature one needs to become conscious of these invisible a priori facts - facts which, for all their intangibility, the tangible world nevertheless relies upon and is inconceivable without.

Think for a moment about wheat. The wheat of a particular farm is a finite thing from the point of view of the particular farmer. He has only so much. He thinks of his specific quantity and of its growth and what he will need to sell it for in order to keep his economy going. But if one thinks of all the farmers one begins to think of wheat in an infinite sense. For wheat is always present on the earth, waxing and waning locally as the earth turns, but globally always there. From the point of view of a satellite outside the earth the process of grain production, not the finite quantities of grain themselves, is what matters. One can pass in this way from the specific and finite manifestations of nature into her infinite processes and thus into nature herself. In this way, too, one develops a deeper sense of what nature is. One does not stop short at her outer manifestations only.

The currents of the oceans, the weather, the existence of minerals. Nature consists of realities such as these, independent of the human being, "before" economic life. While it is true that the economic life derives in part from nature, nature is, strictly speaking, outside the economy. In the same sense as the farmer who tills the soil does not create or invent the soil. For him it is a given of his situation.

Nature is one of the boundaries of economic life. The other is spirit. The capacities of the human being are analogous to natural phenomena in that they too represent invisible realities. If one goes beyond the capacities of the individual themselves (the ability for example to carve wood), one can arrive at the processes whereby these capacities come about and then on to the individual inhabiting them, so to speak. In this sense, as a direct reflection of nature, one can deepen one's understanding of what is meant by spirit, and one can arrive at a difficult to name, yet real conception of the spiritual world - that which lies behind and comes to expression in the capacities of the human being.

But the two worlds of nature and of spirit cannot be separate. They are together, held together through the human being who belongs to both. There is another saying: Spirit is never without matter; matter never without spirit. It is a task of our age, no less so for economics, to see these two worlds clearly and in connection with one another. Not to refuse the reality of one in preference for the other, neither fleeing the earth nor going too deep into it. We must stand on the earth while ennobling it through our presence. An economics based on a true conception of nature and spirit will admit to ideas that are sound, if a little less dry than acadmics might like, and these in turn will give rise to ways of doing things that are workable.

## LAND AND CREDIT

Nature and spirit are given far more immediacy in economic terms when one says "land" and "credit", for in reality these categories refer to the same thing. Nature in her largest and specifically economic sense is "land". Not land in particular, but land generally. And economic life takes its start in part from the moment that man begins to work the land, be it through agriculture, mining or any other form of activity.

Man working on the earth transforming its products is one side of economic life. And yet when he is working, the human being is constantly being directed by thought of one kind or another. He is always seeking to be more effective in his work, to get more result from less effort. Underlying the outer phenomenon of work, therefore, is the invisible one of constant betterment. In fact the evolution of consciousness is based on man bettering his ideas through working on matter. The two are inextricable. How could an artist produce a masterpiece, if not at the end of his apprenticeship? How could the clods of earth become anything more noble or complex were it not for the ingenuity of man working upon them? The elaboration of nature is based on the application and development of capacities. These capacities cannot be developed otherwise than by working on nature. The two worlds (of work and capacities, nature and spirit) are distinguishable in the mind, but not in reality.

But why "land" and why "credit"? Land and credit are two economic categories - not yet the physical things of economic life, but concepts, realities whereby we can get to grips with economic life. For whereas one cannot escape the reality of the worlds of nature and of spirit, they remain abstractions in the main and need to be grounded, connected to the outer, separate phenomena of the world.

Land is nature in its physical entirety - all land that men can or do work upon to produce the products of the earth. Everything in economic life in the way of goods, even the coinage and paper of money itself, has been made out of the land. Land in this sense is truly representative of nature.

I think the idea is clear. What is not so clear is that it is very easy to give preference to land over the intangible aspects of life, precisely because it is so tangible and obvious. But from this point of view one runs the real danger of seeing anything else as of a lesser order and, more important, of not giving credence to the spirit in its economic sense. Everything becomes subservient to land.

But this is a life untruth. There could be no transformation of the land, were the human being not activated by his capacities as these develop within him and seek expression. Even the farmer is moved by his evolution in the first place, not by the work he does on the land. It is vital to see that the realm of capacities is of equal weight. That neither land nor spirit are primary. The two coexist.

Credit, as the Latin tells us, has to do with believing in people. One believes that a child will develop talents and skills sufficient to base his adult life on and, based on this belief, one funds his education. One extends credit to the growing child precisely because one believes that something will come of him. Credit is advanced by financiers to enable ideas to be realised in the physical world. One advances money on the strength of the idea one wishes to back. The more real the idea, the less the risk run but one is all the time banking on something invisible, something intangible. One may take a charge on the earth, but that is as a backstop. One banks on ideas, physically invisible ideas!

Credit thus represents invisible ideas. It is made good when these ideas become realised and when what was once only in the mind's eye has become a saleable product able to repay the investment in it.

Land and credit, nature and spirit - the two go together.

But now the question becomes: Is there something as representative of land, as land is of nature? And something as representative of credit as credit is of spirit? Things that are very physical and yet epitomise the very unphysical concepts of nature and spirit? Things, indeed, on which to base the world's money.

## OF WHEAT AND GOLD

The essential fact, that economic life derives both from all that comes from nature and all that comes from spirit, can be summed up, albeit a little crudely, in the relationship between agriculture and production of any other kind; the fact that all human activity presupposes man has food to eat and thus is based economically on food production and agriculture generally. This is a relationship that requires careful scrutiny, however, for it is easily misunderstood and there is a need to be wary, in particular, of the idea that agriculture is the basis of all life.

The disecology of modern agri-economics not unnaturally leads men to go back to pre-industrial times when, they are wont to think, life was cosier and economically more stable. A return to agricultural economics is also evocative and provides a haven for the kind of mind which is actually unable to meet the more severe and strict discipline needed to go beyond industrial economics rather than to revert to former times. Romantic ideas about the economics of former times are at odds with the fact that economic life has always been faced with the problem of understanding the relationship between nature and spirit, land and capital. The destabilising factor in recent centuries has been that men have begun to think about this relationship and, insofar as they have not thought it through fully, they have created theories and then practices which are both unstable and destabilising. The unspoken assumption, that before the modern era economic life was stable, overlooks the kind of thinking that has destabilised it. Today a stable economy is above all dependent on the condition of a clear and incisive thinking capable of describing accurately the reality of economic life rather than guessing at it.

No clearer theme could there be to assess one's thinking in this respect than that of the Wheat Theory - the idea that cereal products have formed the basis of all economic activity from time immemorial and will continue to do so. While one cannot doubt that the cereal production of the world is a major factor in economic life and needs, for that reason, to be given full consideration, it is by no means clear, as I hope to indicate, that it is the factor on which all others depend.

The Wheat Theory has been variously stated and includes a number of ideas which sound plausible enough in themselves, but do not necessarily stand closer inspection. For example: the idea that economic equilibrium in the world depends on cereals derives from the thought, that to produce man must first eat and that, therefore, the surplus of food he produces above his own requirements determines the number that can be engaged on non-agricultural activities - industrial production, distribution transport and other services - as well as the volume of industrial and non-food production that can be undertaken. This idea relies on the picture of all nonagricultural activity held in reciprocal relationship to agriculture and suggests that so long as the value of nonagricultural production remains subservient to that of food all will be well. Admittedly this somewhat hopeful expectation is more appealing than mechanistic theories of self-regulating economic relationships, but is it true that agriculture occupies this primary position? After all, men ate long before the ancient Persians learnt the techniques of agriculture. If one is looking for a primary activity it would need to be hunting, or gathering wild foods, rather than farming.

One must be wary of the assumption that agriculture precedes culture itself. Persons actively involved in creative processes are often known to go without food. While it is understandable to argue that physical work requires food, it betrays a clear bias in thinking to place this kind of economic activity above the non-physical. When it comes to creative activity the idea that food comes before all else comes into question. It can equally well be said that creative activity comes before food.

In saying this I am hinting at my own thesis, namely, that it is too simple to insist that modern economics needs to get back to a cereal standard. The problem is to understand the relation between physical and creative activity - both of which arise in every human being and are not in any real sense the characteristics of separate and distinct classes. It is rather simplistic to seek to make either of these factors king of the castle. The obvious need is to synthesise the two, giving each its due and recognising where their contrast leads to. This is not to argue against a cereal standard, but it is to ask:- What is needed in addition to a cereal standard?

It will lead nowhere to say that there should be a wheat standard rather than a gold standard, for example. Certainly the role of wheat in the world economy needs to be properly understood, but little purpose is served by suggesting that the gold standard is an interloper. The question is:- What lies behind the gold standard? To what does gold point? Gold is after all, as much a part of nature as are cereals, although admittedly of a different order.

The gold standard came about in the eighteenth century in England at a time when money and commodities were becoming divorced from one another. The development of economic life toward a world economy was a major influence in this process, but more direct origins of the gold standard can be attributed to John Locke, Lord Summers and others, who were active in the guidance of the economic life of the day. As they struggled to meet the circumstances of their era, they decided on a definite equation between sterling, the national unit of account, and gold of a fixed weight and standard. The price of gold to that of silver was set at a higher ratio than on the Continent with the result that in the first half of the eighteenth century there was an efflux of silver out of and a corresponding influx of gold into Britain. The cereal standard was driven out in consequence. Unaware that his difficulties arose from this intrusion of the precious metal standard into the cereal standard, Sir Isaac Newton, then Master of the Mint, found Locke's conception of a fixed Mint parity for gold and silver troublesome in practice, and so gold was adopted as a standard for want of a better. It was the practical financier's answer to an economic problem that none knew how to solve. The rate set by Newton (1oz. gold = £4 4s 111/2d) held for two centuries, which says something both about the acumen that practicality can bring, but also about the powerful position Britain held in those times. The triumph of the gold standard was strengthened by legislation, particularly the 1816 Act in Britain and other events at the end of the Napoleonic time, and its prestige was finally sealed by Sir Robert Peel in the Bank Charter Act of 1844 (followed by the repeal of the Corn Laws in 1846).

The basis of the gold standard is, however, arbitrary in that it is held in situ, not by biological facts, as one might call them, but by legal arrangements. Such things as the equation of a fixed weight and fineness of gold with a fixed amount of paper money; the restriction of currency value within certain limits determined by the quantity of gold in the central bank; definite promises to pay gold on demand. Moreover, each nation had different rules. But the one factor common to all was the issue of paper money far in excess of actual gold reserves and the fervent hope that conversion demands for gold in exchange for paper currency would remain within the arbitrary limits assigned by law.

Arbitrary law and fond hope are all very well, however, and should not be dismissed out of hand when it comes to practical management of the economy, but they can be, and often are, at odds with life itself. At such times, it is pointless to insist that convention prevail over the weight and flow of evolution. The new circumstances have to be accurately described and existing arrangements modified to accommodate them.

Despite the shortcomings that this brief synopsis points up, the important thing to note is the process of abstraction whereby money passes from grain to metals to paper to credit. Given this evolution, it simply does not do to see grain as sacrosanct. Far more important is it to ask what is the difference between the ancient grain-based and the modern credit-based economy?

The chief difference lies in the fact that man's consciousness has changed. Man has emancipated himself from nature and cannot return within her matrix. The point is that man has to master nature and take her evolution forward. In economics this means that credit must find a relationship with nature.

It is increasingly the case that man has to determine the value of economic life; this can no longer be governed automatically. Neither by nature nor by mechanistic devices such as gold standards and central bank interest rates. It is not unreal and certainly not wrong to create credit. The problem is knowing what credit is in relation to that which proceeds from nature. And here only man can judge and decide. The relationship is reciprocal but it is not finite. I do not think, for example, that the ratio of gold reserves to currency is arbitrary. Men have decided on it, to be sure, but it is something their experience guided them in. Certainly, human experience is fraught with unclear understanding and questionable motives, but that simply argues for a sharpening of economic consciousness and a lessening of egoism in economic affairs. It does not argue against the gold standard, or against credit as such.

Indeed, it has been suggested that gold stocks should be used as a medium of monetary control, itself controlled by the fluctuations in world agricultural production. In terms of this idea the gold cover of the note issues of all the central banks of the world would be comprised in an international monetary mechanism whereby they were moved or were forced or allowed to move in conjunction with the long-term fluctuations of world production and stocks of foodstuffs. Could it be, therefore, that there should be both a wheat standard and a gold standard?

# 3: WHEAT AND GOLD

## GOLD

I know that there are many today who reckon gold to have lost its significance in economic life, but to my mind this could only be the case if, in times of adversity, men no longer took refuge in gold. The powerful psychology of gold is based on an immutable fact of life namely, its physical properties and its universality. Nothing compares to gold. The value of gold in monetary terms varies, of course, with the value men put on it. This value today varies with the role ascribed to gold. If gold is not considered important, as is the current orthodoxy, obviously its value is diminished. But if gold really had no economic meaning, South Africa would lose much of its world importance and the banks would not jealously guard their gold stocks. This, however, is hardly the situation today, so one must view with some skepticism the idea that gold no longer has relevance.

In an economy (or in economic circumstances) where circulation is in full tilt, there is little thought of gold so long as the real things, the consumable things in life remain readily available. But when they do not, when real things become scarce, men resort to gold precisely because it is not consumable. Gold is permanent. It cannot be consumed. It can only be redistributed. It can be lumped together or finely dispersed, concentrated or extended, but it cannot be destroyed.

In this there is an important picture. The fortunes of man's economic life are also subject to contraction and expansion. As an economy contracts, so there is an inevitable tendency to concentrate on gold. If the economy were to stop and start again, those who held gold would be the ones best able to resume trading because gold is pan-economic. We need to understand this relationship. It is fundamental to the psychology of economics that when things get tight, men go for gold. When things ease up, men relax their grip on the precious metal. Gold, accordingly, increases and decreases in value.(1)

Gold mediates between universal, physical and cosmic facts and the human soul. When not in possession of it (perhaps one could equally well say, when not possessed by it), one can enter into this relationship. One's mind is not clouded by possession. Gold when used, rather than possessed, is released into the economy to generate circulation (expand trade) and removed to slow it down. It is thus the balancer. That is what the Ancients knew when they administered, but did not possess, gold. Gold was kept in but not of the economy. Of the economy it is poisonous. In it it is healing.

When gold is of the economy, the depths men will go to get it are well illustrated by the depth of the mines in South Africa (3,000 metres), the ratio of gold extracted from ore mined (1:156,800), the lowness of wages paid to gold miners, and the depths below ground of the storage vaults into which the dug-up gold is then buried again! These are telling pictures, indicative phenomena.

Gold needs to be seen to be behind rather than within the overall economy. Its value rises as the economy shrinks (circulation slows); decreases as trade expands (circulation speeds up). This illustrates the role of gold - as a kind of thermometer or barometer of economic life. Unlike the mercury in the thermometer, however, gold's deliberate introduction into or withdrawal from circulation directly affects the economy. The analogy to mercury in the thermometer breaks down, because economics is both an ethical and a practical science. For this reason also, the true nature of gold and its true role in economic life cannot be made apparent unless gold is removed from external trade (except for the purposes of ornamentation, industrial applications and the like), and its use confined to balancing the economy by way of being on temporary loan, as it were.

Gold is a remarkable substance. A description of its physical properties can leave one in awe. Gold is present everywhere on the earth in the seas, in the highest strata of the atmosphere and in the earth itself on every continent. It exists as the finest dust and in dense nuggets. There are, however, no veins of gold as there are of other metals. The denser deposits are combined with silica, for example, or in iron or sulphur compounds containing arsenic. Combined with silver, mercury, copper and antimony, however, gold is to be found finely distributed.

Gold has a special affinity to light, radiating it rather than retaining it. This quality is the reason for its use in the wonderful colours of stained glass and other treasured artifacts. But it is light-related also in terms of weight, being capable of transformation into the thinnest of gold leaf, more delicate than butterfly wings. On the other hand, gold is the heaviest substance known, its specific gravity of 19.3 compares to lead's 11.6.

It does not oxidise or combine with any other substance except potassium cyanide. It remains unto itself. Gold is the most extensible substance on earth - one gramme can be extended into a thread nearly two kilometres long - and yet a 2mm thickness can withstand a tractive power of 60 kilogrammes.

By its very nature gold mediates between infinite expansion and strong cohesion, between dispersion and hardening. And because of its contrasting properties gold is extraordinarily stable. Its economic significance is a direct echo of its physical nature. The ability of gold to pass back and forth between extremes is a perfect corollary of the healthy circulation of values between tangibility and intangibility that this essay is all about.(2)

Because of its physical properties, gold affords us permanent value. It is the substance par excellence that represents circulation. If one were to mint the coinage of a true money one could not be more precise in one's choice of metal than to choose gold. Gold's chief characteristic, economically speaking, is that it cannot be destroyed. It cannot be consumed. Nor can it be made, not even by alchemy. All one can do with gold is redistribute it. One can do this by digging it up, melting it down, exchanging it and so on. But one can do, and one does, nothing else with gold except redistribute it. Circulation in very physical fact.

Gold has a changing value, of course, in the sense of what men are prepared to pay for it or what they think it will buy. This depends on the vagaries of human deeds. But, irrespective of its value in that sense, gold has immutable weight. It is traded by the Troy ounce. What, however, is the Troy ounce? 480 grains of wheat!

Gold, this royal substance that reigns supremely over all economic life regardless of human foibles, points directly to wheat, but why?

---

(1) I am speaking in real economic terms. This is a different matter to that of the nominal or superficial values of gold created by external gold trading. The denominated value of gold is secondary to the value it has over against what it can be exchanged for.

(2) For a fuller discussion of gold, see "History of Money", Gerard Klockenbring, New Economy Publications, 1985.

## WHEAT

For long ages, wheat has been regarded as the foundation of all prices, determinative of the price of other cereals and of all other products in turn. If one sought a currency based only on physical consumable commodities, one would be well advised to choose wheat.

Two vital physical properties of wheat provide the reason why. Two properties seemingly as immutable and stable as those of gold itself. First, it has been observed that good and bad harvests balance each other out over long periods of time, so that one can speak of an average constant harvest.

By identifying this constant one can husband grain resources in order to translate erratic provision into constant supply. Wheat production in a global sense represents a constant in economic life, in just the same way as does the impossibility of creating or destroying gold.

More than this, irrespective of the goodness or badness of the wheat and the consequent fullness or paucity of the single ear, the grains at the centre of the ear have a uniformity of size and weight. It is this constant factor in the wheat grain itself (with the possible exception of modern artificially manipulated hybrids) that has resulted in gold's denomination by wheat since ancient times until today. 1 Troy ounce of gold is equivalent to 480 grains of wheat.

In other words, mint a gold coin of a weight of 1 Troy ounce and emboss upon it a picture of wheat with the figures and words "480 grains wheat" and one has struck the coinage of true money.

## WHEAT AND GOLD

There, in the physical world, independent of the acrobatics and speculative voyages of human reason, quietly awaiting our tranquil observation of it, is the most fundamental economic relationship of all time. A relationship that may yet instil the degree of humility necessary in our minds, in order for us to perceive, as opposed to invent, what true money is all about. In order for money to be true to the enduring realities of economic life it must be denominated in terms of wheat and gold.

Those who reintroduced the Gold Standard in 1816 may or may not have been aware that in doing so they were vanquishing the agrarian economy of old with its effective wheat standards. Commerce prevailed. Man had emancipated himself from mere peasanthood. In the 1930's, when debate was heated over the efficacy or otherwise of the Gold Standard, there was a renaissance of wheat theories, but Keynes's fertile mind, World War II, Bretton Woods and other events in recent history combined to eclipse the light the wheat theorists sought to shed on world finance. Though not the Gold Standard exactly, gold still kept its central position and did so until 15th August 1971, when the USA severed the dollar from gold. In consequence, wheat theorists seem to have dropped entirely out of the picture Even those who seek an "honest money" tend to neglect wheat as the basis of the currency, in favour of the idea of a basket of commodities.

In the last ten years or so mainstream economists have been amusing themselves with clever concepts such as SDR's, petrodollars and ECUs, but wheat has never been given serious consideration. And gold has been officially ruled out. I say "officially", because the banks' gold hoardings on 15th August 1971 amounted to some 36,000 tons, not an ounce of which did they relinquish! A hedge, perhaps, against the possible invalidation of the new orthodoxy?

Leaving aside considerations of vested interests that may or may not be real obstacles to the search for a true money, economists seem always to have supposed gold and wheat to be in opposition to each other. One either leaves agrarian economy in favour of the gold standard; or one discounts gold and opts for a wheat standard. But the relationship between wheat and gold already described seems to cut through this idea, pointing instead directly to the idea of a money standard comprising both wheat and gold.

## FROM COINS TO WORLD TRADE

The coinage of true money has already been described. But the use of coinage is increasingly limited in today's society and one needs to consider whether wheat is capable of more abstract expression. To understand how it could be one needs to survey briefly the history of money.

There was, and in various parts of the world still is, a time when money took the form of actual goods surplus to requirements - cows, shells, and so on. The inconvenience of this form of wealth was, and is, overcome in the course of time by its substitution first with metal coinage of equivalent intrinsic value, then of equivalent face value, and then of equivalent numerical value. Coinage in turn gave, and continues to give, way to paper; and paper to book entries.

In this long process one can observe - once more as a direct expression of the individuation of man - the abstraction or emancipation of money from its being tied to physical substance to its becoming divorced from it. The form of money that we call a book entry is tied to physical matter only by the ink it is written with and the paper it is written on. Moreover, by thinking, the book entry itself can be removed entirely from the physical plane and become a figure in the mind. One can indicate this in the following way.

Having arrived at the abstract form of book entries, and leaving entirely to one side for the moment the problems of usurious money whereby money, or a part of it, represents no real values, one has an entry that says

£lOO.

This figure with its denomination in pounds sterling has an immediate significance. As does $100, 100F, etc. The significance is provided by the denomination, however, not by the figures.

100 on its own means nothing at all. 100 what?

Set aside the national currency symbol, as one would have to in any search for a world money, for example, and one has only figures. The most abstract form of money possible. Pure thought, in effect. To give such money any significance it has to be reclothed in things that connect both it and our consciousness of it to the earth once again.

Suppose the following:

100 = 100 Troy oz of gold or 48,000 grains of wheat.

Neither of these measures or denominations is national. Both have universal, worldwide significance. It is precisely at the point of its greatest abstraction and fullest emancipation that money can be immediately and universally denominated in world terms - above and beyond all the false frontiers that our modern notions of national state economies have set up and which befuddle our minds and bewilder our trade.

It is quite possible for world trade to be conducted in terms of wheat and gold values. Trade is a matter of balancing values so that 100 remains exchangeable for 100. The one hundred may comprise 50 houses, 2 cars and 48 screwdrivers on one side; a ton of wheat, a fishing boat and 98 washing machines on the other. But if one supplies 100 and the other can supply only 84, the 16 has to be made up in some way. 16 can merely remain owing, of course. But if circumstances require it to be cashed in, a form of good will be needed that transcends all others and can be used as a go-between for them all.

A money based on wheat and gold would belong both to the micro economy and to the macro economy. To both local exchange, where coinage tends to be used, as well as international exchange, where trade balances are the medium.

In the macro-economic world such balances would boil down in practice to exchanges in wheat and gold. Traders would be required to husband reserves of gold and wheat for this purpose, the values of which would rise and fall depending on the degree to which they were used to balance and, therefore, to avoid the interruption of trade.

## OUTSIDE THE ECONOMY

The features of gold and wheat pointed out earlier can be said to be meta-economic. Like the sun, they preexist economic life and economic theory, both of which are the truer the closer they follow the nature of the intrinsic meta-economic facts that are to be found imprinted, as it were, in the physical world. Gold and wheat can be said to be outside the economic process; the economic process unfolds and takes its course between the two.

To reflect this in structural terms one need but cease normal trading in both wheat and gold, declare them both man's common wealth and the cover for the world's money, and place their worldwide distribution in the hands of special commissions, a wheat and a gold authority, whose sole task would be to administer them as the basis of the world's currency. Gold would still be available for decorative usage, as would wheat for making into bread, but neither would be available for the purpose of private gains merely to be made by the withholding and releasing of stocks from and into world markets as the prices rose and fell according to one's manipulations.

No doubt, many people would, will and do oppose such ideas, let alone any actual measures to introduce them into practical life. Such bridges should be crossed as one gets to them, however, and it is perhaps more important at this stage to consider those aspects of life that would be ameliorated by what is being suggested in this essay. For example, to the degree that social inequalities in South Africa are due to a struggle over gold ownership, the tension there would be relaxed by such developments. The nonsense of moving 160,000 tons of earth to get out one ton of gold could be done away with, and those who spend their lives in the bowels of the earth for little gain to themselves would be allowed a life more worthy of the human being. The need to know how much gold Russia has, and the supposed ignorance in this matter (despite satellites that can tell us whether people in Siberia are dining with their lights on or off) would be consigned to the waste bin of so much fruitless politicking and wasteful squabble. Huge mountains of grain would not need to be kept in bulldozed heaps in London to support wheat prices, while Ethiopians starved and mid-Western farmers went bust. Nor would wheat need to be dumped out at sea, as if humanity were a tyrant who preferred to feed his goldfish rather than his family.

## A MONEY COMMISSION

The two organisations of a Wheat Authority and a Gold Authority would in practice be the two departments of a third, over-arching body - a Money Commission independent of both governmental and financial vested interests. Apart from their separate and specific duties of administering the world's supply of wheat and gold, the two authorities would compare notes and, by direction of the Money Commission, would exchange each other's reserves as necessary to maintain economic stability - that is to say, continuous trade, sufficiently financed. These transactions would be almost entirely book entries; only in rare and special circumstances would wheat and gold need to change hands in a physical sense; just as it is rare today for gold reserves to be shipped to their owners. Certificated entitlement to such reserves by and large replaces physical possession of them.

The Money Commission would have as its main task to ensure that the availability of money at all times matched the values current in the economy. It would not do this by simplistic decrees to the effect that:"Thou shalt have 100% physical cover". It would recognise the need to expand the concept of cover to include the factor of higher credit ratios than 1: 1, as well as the need on occasion to deliberately place a charge on future productivity. But none of these measures would be undertaken by accident, chaotically, or merely because they were technically possible. They would be a concerted action of all three bodies, undertaken each in the light of the other in order to achieve one end only - stable prices, maintained trade, and sound moneys Speculation, usury and economic grand larceny would be outlawed insofar as men sought to practise these "arts" in the medium of the world's money, humanity's common wealth.

What opposes the introduction of a Money Commission? Provided one is disposed at least to entertain the idea, one can arrive quite quickly at the necessary theoretical and empirical starting point for setting it. up. Nor need one be afraid to take the plunge for lack of experience of such things. By its nature such a development in monetary management needs to a certain extent to be discovered in the doing of it. Moreover, the arguments against taking such a step are empty when they suggest it would amount to irresponsible tampering with the workings of the economy. It can hardly be claimed that current economic orthodoxies are grounded in clear theory, or that they are a triumph of practical working! To be sure there are many economists, politicians and even businessmen whose career plans and images of themselves could not withstand a shift of the prevailing paradigm, but this amounts to a vested interest in the status quo, not a cogent argument against a Money Commission.

There is, of course, the immense power of the banks. Quite by whom, how and when this problem will be overcome is something about which one should perhaps keep one's counsel. There can be little doubt, however, that it will require enormous personal courage and sacrifice on the part of those who undertake such a Davidian enterprise, and that it is probably inconceivable and unrealisable in practice without the passage of an Act of Parliament or its equivalent.

But do vested interests and the power of the banks constitute the only, even the most powerful obstacle to the establishment of a Money Commission? I think not. I think there is a less obvious, but more structural hindrance - namely, an inadequate analysis of the significance of credit and, therefore, currencies.

I do not mean to say that the sacred cow of monetary reform is just an ordinary old heifer, to coin a phrase, but she is in danger of being milked dry. One can take the "money equals commodities" idea too far. Over-immersion in this idea can cause the phenomena of credit to appear as a threat to economic stability. There can be no doubt that credit places the value of money at risk when money stands proxy for goods only. And within the realms of credit, it is quite clear that credit created with a view to profiting therefrom and charged against the goods base of the economy constitutes a permanent force against economic stability. In all this the arguments against the creation of credit by private banks are well versed and well rehearsed.

But were there to be a goods-based money managed by a Commission, would the expected economic stability come about? Would basic commodities provide a standard as effective as the gold standard was (in the days when it was effective!) and as effective as the commodity-tied economy that preceded it? Would it, above all, result in a waning of the speculative motive among men - a motive that is often maligned and, indeed, frequently applied antisocially, but which nonetheless is a real force in modern man's make-up. I suspect that much of the opposition to a commodity money is deeply, albeit unconsciously, rooted in the feeling that it does not reckon with this aspect of the human condition. Were the movement for a Money Commission to retrace its footsteps on this point, I believe it would remove a real impediment from within its own theoretical base and in terms of how it is perceived by others.

The reality cannot be escaped that the economy depends on the goods it produces and that fundamental to these is wheat. Indeed, among commodities wheat singles itself out as the basic commodity on which to found a currency standard. But I do not need to repeat wheat-standard theory here. What seems to go unrecognised is that physical goods are only one pole of economic life. The other is human ingenuity.

Wheat, as any other good, presupposes the wisdom of the farmer his many judgments, decisions, and efforts to improve his efficiency. Whereas one can say, correctly, that future economic activity is a charge on the existing asset base; one can also say that the existing asset base is a result of such activity. Every credit has a corresponding debit. To credit a new venture is to debit the existing economy. But the converse is also true. Assets are a credit only because of what they owe to entrepreneurial initiative and human ingenuity generally.

It was, and continues to be, an error of thought to oppose credit and commodities, gold and wheat. The rise of capitalism, as its name implies, presented man with a new experience - human ingenuity in economic affairs unfettered by mediaeval mores and social relationships. Imagining a new future (speculating!) became a cultural phenomenon and required forms of credit that transcended physical goods. At this point the need was and, I believe, continues to be, to complement the wheat standard, such at it was, with a gold standard. Untold confusion has been created by attempting to replace the one with the other, because although it is necessarily influenced by existing physical goods, human ingenuity is not determined by them. Gold cannot be a standard for physical goods any more than wheat (or commodities generally) can be a measure of human ingenuity and inventiveness.

What is needed, even today, is a dual standard of wheat and gold. The price of goods needs to be seen and thus held in relation to basic commodity prices, the most basic being wheat. But the price of credit needs to be seen to belong to gold. To make this step one needs only to understand that the basic and most powerful economic significance of gold is not its availability - either in abstract terms of world-wide deposits or in relative terms as when, for example, it has flooded the European economy - but its durability and the fact that it cannot be destroyed.

Not until each is given its due can the warfare be ended between goods and credit, wheat and gold. The introduction of a dual standard of wheat and gold will prevent the needs of credit from debasing the value of the physical economy; but it will also enable the movement for a Money Commission to lie with the grain of the modern human condition by steering it past the confusion of making credit conditional on the existing physical economy.

A dual currency standard of wheat and gold would transform the context and mode of operation of today's economy because, in addition to the need for Money Commissions - ultimately on a worldwide basis - it would speak of the need to remove both wheat and gold from normal trading and to treat both as regulating elements money, in other words.

The workings of the Federal Reserve System in America provide valuable study material in this connection. The FRS was created by Congress in 1913 but is run by the 12 regional Federal Reserve Banks and their commercial member banks. Its stock is held by its member banks and its staff are not part of the Civil Service. The FRS is governed by a Board of Governors, appointed by the President and confirmed by the Senate, together with a Federal Advisory Council (made up of directors of the regional banks) and a Federal Open Market

Committee. The FRS operates without the participation of the President, Congress or Treasury. Its policy is formulated by the Open Market Committee, whose decisions are in fact "operations", that is, instructions to purchase or sell government or other securities (securities being promises to meet their given values).

The FRS purchase of securities (by self-created, uncharged credit) increases money supply; sale (by destruction of credit) decreases money supply. In this way federal reserves are generated or extinguished and thus the banking system's overall capacity to lend is maintained.

There are many questions about 'The Fed'. For example, couldn't the large charge it places on tax revenues be avoided altogether if the Government itself created debt-free credit instead of the FRS? And one can question who should control the workings of the system and to what end. But if one sets these questions to one side, one can see - without any real contention - the clear process whereby the wherewithal to finance the economy is made possible by managing the money supply commensurately with the value of available goods and services.

This function should not be carried on for profit, however, because it is regulatory of the economy and not productive of values. The credit or reserves thus created should, as in the FRS, be created as necessary. However, such values should not be *given* into the economy but lent - advanced and withdrawn solely to provide liquidity for existing values, not to augment or diminish these values. The strict purpose needs to be adhered to of facilitating the circulation of values, without causing, hindering or falsifying the process whereby they come about or get used up.

# 4: USURY AND WASTE

## USURY

The establishment of a Money Commission comprising both Wheat and Gold Authorities would completely transform the landscape of social and economic life. The main features of this new environment can be fairly easily identified,although whether humanity will ever populate it is another matter!

Perhaps the first and most obvious feature of this new landscape is the revised role of the banks. The banks today enjoy a position and power that many people find questionable. Operating as private and commercial undertakings, charged with making a profit for their investors, they make financing their business. Now it needs to be recognised that it is one thing to provide credit at an interest level sufficient to cover the costs of doing so, and another to charge the highest level possible. The difference is where the banks make their profits, of course, but since time immemorial this difference has been considered usurious.

In the Middle Ages and before, as indeed in certain areas of the world today, usury was forbidden (which is not to say that it didn't happen, of course). It was forbidden by religious authorities in a time when it was they who largely directed human society. This condition having passed away in most of the world, the stop was taken off usury. It is quite unfashionable to raise the matter today and archaic to press it. Nevertheless it is essential to understand what usury is and why it is a problem. In olden times the whole issue was bound up with moral laws given from above or outside and requiring obedience, not explanation. Today the matter of usury can be described in straightforward economic terms. Whether one sees in it a moral issue or not is left to the individual.

Suppose one wishes to sell something, say a chair. One need's to sell it to get money to pay the rent. One finds a buyer, who gives some money for it and, relieved, one banks it with instructions to the bank to pay the landlord. The banker tests the money and finds that it is counterfeit. One has exchanged something for nothing, been robbed. The other person has received something for nothing. That is the essence of usury. And it can take many forms, blatant or subtle, intended or unwilling. From a moral point of view make of it what one will; but economically its effect is clear. False values are introduced into the economy by usury, and these debase the values already there. Inflation is a direct outcome, as the price of goods tries to equate with the value of money in the economy, unaware that some of this money is fictitious.

In real terms, usury was outlawed because it was uneconomic. The question today is whether it should continue to be. If one is seeking a true form of money, then usury must be ruled out. But to do this money itself must be kept out of the trading process; it must be maintained as a representative of real values and prevented from becoming their substitute.

## USURIOUS BANKING

Modern banking is usurious to the extent that it makes money out of financing activities. The problem is less the fact that banks generate credit the value of credit is more a function of its cover, than of who issues it - than that they lend, or to be more exact, sell, this credit at a higher price. It is inevitable that a choice has to be made in this matter either to continue with usurious practices and forever fight the fires thus ignited and fuelled; or cease it, and sort out whatever adjustments are necessary to one's psychology, cash flow and hunger for power! One could outlaw usury from a moral standpoint - as Islam does, for example - or one could create sufficient popular pressure to do so by direct legal measures, as some monetary reformers advocate. Public support for such measures, however, would tend to require strong evidence that the economic consequences would be overwhelmingly advantageous. It is probably most fruitful, therefore, to try to realise the required change in economic terms - by demonstrating, or letting life itself demonstrate, that usury is uneconomic and expensive and that it disguises its real effects by inflating the reference point while it devalues the currency. What good are colossal gains in property or farming, for example, if they are achieved by processes that inflate the values to a point where they suddenly go in reverse? Surely a steady modest level would be better than soaring heights, suddenly discounted, only to soar again?

The deflation of the economy and the downscaling of banking activity by the amount that it is usurious would not affect the mechanics of banking in any way. It would affect the power and the self-prestige of bankers, the profit strategies of speculators and so on - but that is a separate matter. The world envisaged with a world money based on wheat and gold is one in which a full range of banking facilities from the most primitive changing of a £10 note for ten £1 coins, to the most sophisticated fund management - would remain. The management of the world's money would, however, be under the direction of the Money Commission and would not be the subject or source of profit, least of all the profit of those responsible for its management.

Given that huge vested interests do and will continue to oppose any such development, a grass roots approach probably has more mileage than any other. Local experiments and wherever possible permanent arrangements should be encouraged - and in any event seem to be happening spontaneously. Apart from their immediate local effects, which tend to be to reconnect money to people and their local economic life, these endeavours - where they are not stopped by antithetical interests - have the effect of shrinking the area in which usurious banking operates. A head-on political battle without the electoral and empirical support of such endeavours is likely to be quixotic.

As regards the political front more specifically, the many new parties - be they green or not so green - all seem to lack an economic dimension. To that extent they may well prove toothless in the real world. On the other hand, for example, political strategies that are centred on ecology and responsible concern over nuclear power should find a ready ally in the movement for monetary reform, especially since the ruination of the earth - a cause they have in common is a direct effect of the usurious money of our times.

## WORLD AND NATIONAL DEBT

One major effect of a Money Commission administering wheat-gold money would be that the manipulation of the world economy by banks as part of political and/or commercial strategies would have no place. The world debt problems of today would not, could not arise. Financing world trade and economic development would be done strictly in conformity with the inherent economic possibilities of the places concerned, not merely as extensions of the corporate or political objectives of banking corporations or foreign governments. The IMF and similar institutions would find themselves with a genuine role to play in world finance, or out of a job. The World Bank might truly justify its name, or battle to preserve its present functions of acting on behalf of the imperialistic forces that underlie Western money. The hidden economy of Russia would be uncovered. Aid programmes with their pretence at being apolitical would have to put their money where their mouths were. The patent nonsense would fall away of trying to preserve nation-state economies when everywhere the facts speak otherwise. To the extent that a Japan wanted to be a major force in world economics, rather than an extension of Western money, she could and would be. The imminent effect of a China entering the world economy in a powerful way would not need to chill the hearts of those who have stashed their cash in Hong Kong, or invested heavily in Taiwan. In short, the world would cease to be experienced as an economic battleground, but become a place in which humanity cooperated, dividing the labour and benefits within itself equitably (which does not mean equally) and for the good of all.

Key to such changes would be the transformation of the National Debt - in idea and in practice. This transaction, whereby the State borrows money privately at interest, has long been challenged. Ever since William Paterson and his colleagues settled their score with Charles I and Charles II, National Debts have plagued the world. A Money Commission, such as envisaged here, would be neither a state nor a commercial body. It would be similar to the judiciary - a kind of cultural institution making judgments for the good of all, not for its own sake. The State would have to make legal provision for such a commission, and the commercial banks would remain as those who handled the world's money - albeit for a fee to cover operating costs plus a non-usurious profit - but the Commission itself would belong to neither.

## PEACEFUL MONEY

"Too far-reaching." "Fantastic." "Impossible to achieve." These are the typical criticisms levelled at monetary reforms. They come, of course, from those who stand to lose from reform and their intellectual merit is flimsy, belonging as it does to the economics that is responsible for the very chaos and economic suffering that monetary reform sets out to alleviate.

What such criticisms overlook is the underlying motive of monetary reform to restore order into the world's finances so as to preserve and further the human freedom that is dependent upon it. Be it the use of "structural adjustment" policies or hypocrisy in regard to sanctions, the squabblings of the European Union, or the long-term, staunch but then sudden withdrawal of support for Persia's Shah, the Philippines' Marcos or Haiti's Duvalier, the West has a clear record of dishonest and duplicitous conduct. Those who criticise the West and who are perceived as a threat to it, often as not point to her moral bankruptcy. The failure of capitalism to deal with the inequities created or existent in its own dominions and their exportation to other economic regions - this is the lameness that non-Westerners observe.

While the idea of a Money Commission certainly puts in jeopardy and seeks to replace those whose involvement in world finance is for anything less than genuine world economic stability and equitable distribution of wealth, it does so only because it is intended to avert moral bankruptcy (which only sophisticated footwork is currently able to keep at bay) or the *cause celebre* of crusades against the West from political or religious movements inimical to the true freedom of the individual.

Much is said these days about nuclear weaponry as the real reason for world peace in recent times. This remark is quite inaccurate, of course. What is meant is that another world war has yet to take place and that so far fifty years have elapsed since the end of World War II, which is more than twice the period after 1918. But that is not the point. Since 1946 the world has been in constant military turmoil. And even if the major powers have avoided direct confrontations, it can hardly be claimed that they have been uninvolved in these events. Nuclear weapons have meant nothing in Indochina, Africa, Iran, Poland, Hungary, Czechoslovakia, Northern Ireland, Spain, South America and so on. True world peace cannot be guaranteed by military arms, any more than the Pope can achieve it through his Jesuitical language of a "battle for peace". Introduce a true form of money, on the other hand, and peace will be a natural outcome.

## WASTE ECONOMICS

Peace? Who wants peace?! The economic effect of peace would be the cessation of defence and armaments expenditure! Those who talk in illusions about four decades of world peace ought to look more carefully at the economics of the military. Add up the cost of military economics in our time and imagine its redeployment in peaceful enterprises, such as feeding people, educating them and generally lessening the inequities of life. In this way the true nature of modern peace can be seen. Admittedly, starvation when the rest of the world throws food away is not the conventional meaning of war. But violence need not only be ballistic in kind.

What about the economics of waste more generally? Goods that wear out quickly. Parts that are replaced, not mended, and that often necessitate the replacement of other, perfectly good, ones - to which they are welded, instead of screwed. What about the wasted resources of endless packaging, unrecycled paper and so on? Resources that are wasted - both in the sense that refuse is thrown away, and that forests are denuded to satisfy the needs of our voracious waste bins? Where is the sense in all this? So much wasted effort, wasted time, wasted lives. Modern man keeps going economically only due to the phenomenon of huge surpluses, not due to the wisdom of his own actions.

Apart from the belligerent and selfish motives and productivities of man that these things represent, they also tell another, more important story. The economic conditions of today are those of abundance, not scarcity. Surpluses are created far greater than we actually need. In specific economic terms, we could all work less and do as well. These surpluses need to disappear - to be used up. Modern money does this in two ways - *physically* it creates products whose real purpose is to be thrown away; *monetarily* it devalues the currency. Waste economics is the direct and inevitable result of usurious money. In reality money cannot represent nothing. When it is introduced as nothing, actual goods must be thrown away in order to restore economic balance. A true form of world money would give quite different expression to this reality. Rather than throw surpluses away, it would need to give them away. In this there is a profound difference.

# 5: THE GIVING OF SURPLUSES

## SURPLUS VALUE

It is, perhaps, difficult to swallow the idea that ours is a time of huge surpluses. We have become familiar with the language of scarcity and austerity, threatening bankruptcy, inflation and devaluation, a raped earth and a fratricidal humanity. In the midst of all this is the devilment worked by those who suggest that the surplus value in the economy is both limited and in dispute as to which class should own it. If ever proof were needed that ideas, not material forces of production, were the most powerful force in economic life, the materialist concept of surplus value would provide it. Seldom has such enormous wastage been attributable to a false idea! By the same token, a correct understanding of surplus value promises to unfold unheard-of wealth - not so much in terms of self-centred riches, but in terms of a more relaxed economic existence and a more expansive attitude to our fellow men. A true form of money would not lead to the idea and practice of everyone trying to amass a physical fortune at others' expense; it would be characterised by the experience that everyone had enough money to finance the things he, according to his own judgment, needed. Shared circulation, not isolated deposits, would be the order of the day.

Surplus value, as it is called, is constantly created through the process of exchange. It accompanies the physical economy, invisibly following its contours. Because it is intrinsic to life man cannot claim credit for its existence, nor can he claim that the surpluses belong to him. They are there for the benefit of humanity as a whole and the nearest they should come to man himself is through the medium of money, circulating in but not being of the economy. If one calculates the full extent of the waste economics of obsolescence, war, space projects and so on, it is easy to see that there is wealth enough for all humanity. It is simply a matter of whether we wish to use this wealth to finance the lives we could be living: free and devoid of drudgery - or whether we prefer to remain shackled and so throw the extra away, burn it up, send it into space or use it to beat each other.

If we could see that surplus value is not for the possession of man then we would not spend our forces in trying to wrest it from one class or another, or persist in the fiction that banks create credit, when in fact all they do is appropriate surpluses.

Surpluses, however, are the most difficult things to understand, precisely because they are invisible and our minds are trained to observe only the physical. No end of confusion results from this fact. Once we can get used to the idea that invisible things are also visible to the mind, albeit in a non-physical way, then we can see surpluses differently.

This is not such a tall order. All economic categories are invisible we take them seriously nevertheless. Who has ever seen a price or a value, inflation or labour? We have seen figures written on labels, experienced our money not buying as much as it did before, and seen men digging ditches. But these are not the same thing.

The modern mind is kidding itself when it refuses to recognise the invisible realities that affect us. Who has seen a worry? Who has seen a headache? A large part of our lives - especially our earthly travail consists precisely in things we definitely experience, but never physically see. The notion that we are materialists is really one that we can ill-afford today. It would be better and more honest to admit that there are invisible aspects to life. One does not even need to engage in complex philosophical debate about this - leave that to those who wish to calculate exactly how many angels there are in heaven. After all such information is secondary to the fact that the angels are there in the first place. It doesn't prove their existence. There is a very subtle point midway between materialist thought that refuses to recognise non-material things, and abstract spiritual conceptions that, in contrast, seek to name them. Between these two there is a silent area wherein the recognition can take place that life is not only physical. Bide awhile in this region and one can overcome the inadequacies of materialist explanations of life without falling prey to the complicated matter of naming the invisible.

Economics, because it concerns everyone, is not helped by the narrow materialistic notions that frequently arise within it. But it is not helped either by an over-specific spiritual terminology. On the other hand, it is given enormous strength from the experiences to be had at the edge, so to speak, of material phenomena. The value of a commodity is not in the thing itself. Values are always in the eye of the beholder. Surplus value is no different.

Once understood in this way, the notion of possessing surplus value, dragging it down into personal ownership, does not arise. Instead, a completely different idea arises, Surplus value appears as something that is, as it were, god-given. Bestowed on humanity by life itself, just as the warmth and light of the sun are.

## THE INDIVIDUATION OF MAN

What is it that creates surplus value in this sense? What is it that results in the permanent circulation of surplus value and that gives rise to huge increases in it from time to time?

Surplus value is created by the individuation of man. Every human being experiences the need to develop, to progress. A day cannot pass without his measuring the degree to which he has, or has not, moved forward. No-one has the aim in life to go backwards. This fact of human psychology lies behind every phenomenon of progress, improvement and betterment. It bears directly on economic life because it is this force in man that constantly seeks to get more out of physical life for the same expenditure of effort. It is this that brings about the division of labour, product improvement, leisure, shorter working weeks, efficiency and a host of other economic categories and expressions. Taken as a whole, and taken as a ceaseless process, this is the origin of surplus value. By its very nature it can be attributed to humanity generally, but not to any particular man or class of men.

This idea cannot be understood, however, unless one also recognises that the human being is in continual process of development and that this is inseparable from his endeavour to be a fully conscious individual in his own right - free and able to think for himself. Independent of the dictates of his parents, teachers, class, bank manager or government. This process of individuation is common to all men. It is a true common denominator. And it is this that, working against the resistance of material life, gives rise to surplus value.

Because this process of individuation works into human life from outside, as it were, the results of it - the surplus value it generates - must return thence also. By its very nature, surplus value must be made to disappear. When we do this by throwing it away or acting destructively, the life we create for ourselves is all the proof we need that this is not the appropriate way to dispose of surplus values. Our experience is quite different when we give our surpluses away - not those we actually need, but those we don't need. And when, as happens from time to time, a major step forward or period of inventiveness comes about such as the Renaissance, the Industrial Revolution or modern computers - then the available surplus value increases proportionately. And since we today live in an age when man can be said to have reached almost the peak of self consciousness and, correspondingly, made the greatest penetration into matter, the size of the surpluses currently available knows no precedent. It is a matter of learning to give money away, rather than throw it away.

## GIVING MONEY

Given that most of us in the West do have more or less what we need, and certainly would have were the usurious element removed from money, it is relatively easy to see that the savings from the overcoming of waste economics, were these redeployed in peaceful enterprise, would go to the benefit of others, to those whose needs were greater. We would be called on to give, rather than aid the "less developed". To provide what others asked for, not what it suited us to let them have. To share and not covet the wealth of the world. In practice, huge sums would need to be given away.

How can this be said? Huge sums are thrown away in wars - what's the difference? Huge sums will have to be wiped off the debt sheets of the world - what's the difference? Think how much better life would be if we gave to a Mexico what we subsequently have to write off? Or how much better off a Mexico would be if we had never extracted our merciless tributes in the first place, only then to return them in empty gestures of false magnanimity.

In addition, therefore, to its denomination in wheat-gold, its administration by a Money Commission independent of political and commercial interests, and its removal from the greedy uses of selfish men, true money would be given away in large amounts. This is no different to the financing of education, for example. Remove private concepts of buying the right to education for one's offspring, and what is educational finance, other than giving away money for the sake of one's child, trusting that he or she will become something. To make one's child repay this sum in his post graduate years would be a nonsense indeed. In our everyday lives we constantly give money away when we get nothing physical in return - cinemas, theatres, holidays, education, medicine. The idea is neither new nor fantastic.

Write it large in macro-economic terms and one can see that for the intangible values of economic life money-- even wheat-gold money will be given, given in the sense that no physical good is received in return.

Without this giving, the surplus value cannot be used up, and merely works to devalue the economic life generally in addition to the physical expression it takes of wastage, munitions, and desecration of the land. The proper giving of surplus values, on the other hand, would maintain the value of economic life and give rise to the physical expression of peaceful economics. Things would not be wantonly wasted; people would not go unfed; and the land would be treated for what it is - the indispensable ground which we all share and on which we all stand and depend for our existence.

# 6: A TASK FOR BRITAIN?

## BRITAIN LOST

Britain today is a country that has no obvious world task - and so it struggles to keep alive its identity with previous prowess. National direction is at best provided by the injunction to "buy British", based on the chancy notion that Britain is an economy unto itself. It never has been, of course, and is certainly not so today. Britain's history is one of trade and when she gave herself the appellation "Great" she did so because of her enormous worldwide influence and activity. But those days are gone. Britain no longer commands great economic heights and admonitions to her people to do so are merely nostalgic. Leading the material economy is not Britain's task today. Ever since the folding up of the British Empire, Britain has been more or less rudderless on the seas of history.

There is a current renaissance of focus on London's money markets, but London will always be one of the world's financial centres. That is a matter of international fact, but it is not a basis for national purpose. To my mind it is difficult to conceive of a direction more truly British than that of economic development - more in the historical sense than pecuniary. The question is only one of the type and direction that true economic development can take today. Trying to make the most of the cheapest goods is not it. And it is nonsense for Britain to emulate the idiosyncratic facts of a Japan or a China. The economy has long since arrived at globality frontiers to which it was largely brought by Britain herself many decades ago. The problem has long been one of understanding what follows this condition.

So long as one has not reached a global economy, there are always other economies with which to trade and vie. Rut the condition of world economy ends this process in terms of a physical geographical expansion. At best it can extend itself out into space, but this development is hardly cheap, efficacious or of much general use. What world economy means is that, in place of the extending of frontiers, the economy needs to awaken to its inherent dynamic. Forward movement in economic life nowadays can only be characterised by unimpeded world trade - and this is only possible if money takes a true form and the surpluses are constantly given away.(3)

In earlier pages, I have tried to outline the nature of economic life and the general effect it has on society. The question that remains to be considered is how wheat-gold money can be given practical expression. How? And where?

---

(3) I do not mean the kind of unhindered trade that GATT/WTO is predicated on. This is not free trade, but freedom of western economic forces to dominate the world economy - a freedom made possible by all manner of direct and indirect interventionism that proceeds under the carefully cultivated cover of free market forces, a notion promoted by countries whose own development was accomplished by anything but free market methods.

## BRITAIN'S CANDIDATURE

The principal feature of a Money Commission (with its two departments administrating wheat and gold) is that it be separate from the influence of commercial interests and beyond the control of political parties serving partisan objectives. Though other countries can no doubt replicate these conditions, Britain, and perhaps England in particular, seems almost to have been "designed" by history for the purpose.

In Britain there is a substantial experience of Commissions, set up by Act of Parliament to be under the Crown but answerable to Parliament. These bodies deliberate and have their remit beyond the reach of commercial or purely political interests and the Commissioners' integrity and lack of beneficial interest can be reinforced by their positions being honorary and or their investment portfolios being subject to restrictions. There is also the judiciary, empowered to make up its own mind, guided by statute law as this is devised, but not directed by it in the matter of judgment. That a man shall be imprisoned for an offence may be statutorily decreed; but it is up to the judge to decide for how long. There is also the National Trust - a body set up by Act of Parliament to own land and property in perpetuity and inalienably for the public benefit. It has a board of trustees, a professional management and membership open to anyone. When taken as a whole, these tried and tested institutions readily suggest synthesis or hybridisation into a body specifically designed to ensure that the world's money remains true - true in its nature, form and denomination, and true to the economic life it represents.

## A NEW POUND STERLING

It is not beyond imagining that an Act of Parliament be passed setting up a Commission for Money, charged with the task of administering the nation's money. A new or special pound could be established for the purpose - being simply a British equivalent or version of the world's money - £1 being given a specific wheat-gold value. Because of the nature of gold and wheat, this special pound (which could just as well displace the present pound) could resume the inner significance of the pound sterling - "sterling" referring to the confidence created by the Hanseatic traders. A New Pound Sterling would stand to contribute much to the stability of the world's money and thus could actually give London an edge on other money markets. For it must not be thought that wheat-gold money is inimical to trade or profit. It is only inimical to usurious economics, in which profits have to be expressed in huge sums because the basic economy is inflationary and unstable. The techniques and machinery of modern economic life would be untouched. It is only the speculative economy that would be affected and any structural changes that derived specifically from its conduct.

The cover for the New Pound Sterling could be provided by investments in reserves of gold and wheat and its stability maintained by the careful administration of these reserves in reference one to another. The technique of doing this would necessitate no new devices~~ nor would the business of doing so need to be taken away from existing gold and wheat organisations. Existing organisations in the field might choose to divest themselves or leave the market, but that would be their decision.

## FICTION OR FANCY?

Fiction or fancy? Perhaps. But a New Pound Sterling would give Britain a quite new economic task. Having brought the world together, so to speak, Britain could go on to harmonise the resulting community. Indeed, there is food for thought in the idea that it is just because Britain washed her hands of any moral or inner follow-up to her imperialism that she is largely responsible for many of the world's modern ills - and her own perhaps most particularly. A practical lead in the field of true money could bring fresh life to an inwardly ailing people and untold benefit to all humanity.

# APPENDIX 1: REAL MONEY

There have been many attempts to establish a "real" or "honest" money. These endeavours have almost all been successful, but have been closed down by legislative means primarily, because their growth would have put in jeopardy the interests of those whose academic positions or whose financial circumstances depended on the idea and working of unreal money. This appendix is not the place to discuss these matters in any depth, but it does serve to draw attention to these endeavours in the field of monetary reform and to illustrate what can be, and is being, done in this area. I have chosen five examples.

In the Channel Isles from 1815 to 1836 there was the Guernsey Market Scheme, whereby local credit was created and used to undertake otherwise "impossible" economic activity and thus to revitalise the town. The traditional banks put a stop to it.(4)

Silvio Gesell, a German businessman who lived for the most part in Argentina, formulated ideas in the 1890s which he had the opportunity to put into practice in 1919. Along with others, he introduced 'Goods Money' ("Wara") into the desperate German economy of the time, generating considerable economic activity and wealth when all around was in chaos and depression. Wara were eventually outlawed by decree in November 1931.(5)

In Austria in the same year the economy of Worgl was reactivated by the issue of "Certified Compensation Bills". Within one year the stagnant economy was reborn, reversing an excess of bank withdrawals over deposits and resulting in the building of many new roads, the planting of forests and other major projects.(6)

More recently, Exeter, New Hampshire in the United States was the scene of an attempt by the well-known economist, Ralph Borsodi, to introduce a "new" kind of money called "constants". Running from June 1972 until January 1974 the Constant was based on a basket of 30 of the world's most important and valuable commodities and worked through checking accounts in a local bank. Here, the scheme ended because of fear that it was an infringement of security issuance laws.(7)

Finally, many successful schemes are currently running all over the World called LETS - Local Exchange Trading System. Using "local money", the members of this scheme trade with one another, computing their services and maintaining their balances at a local office. The scheme runs alongside the normal currency and is convertible into it, but unto itself it is based on the real factors of what the members have contributed to the local economy by way of actual goods made and services rendered.(8)

---

(4) See *How Guernsey beat the Bankers*, Toucan Press, Guernsey 1981.

(5) See *Money, the decisive factor*, Desmond Allhusen and Edward Holloway, Christopher Johnson, London 1959.

(6) Ibid.

(7) Source: *Business Week*, 4 May 1974

(8) Source: *Green Revolution*, Vol 42, No 3, Susan Meeker-Lowry, School of Living, York, Pennsylvania, USA. Also a valuable survey of local currencies can be found in *New Money For Healthy Communities*, Thomas G. Greco Jr., 1994.

# APPENDIX 2: SPECIAL DRAWING RIGHTS

The SDR Scheme was drawn up and approved by the International Monetary Fund in Rio de Janeiro in 1967 and put into effect in January 1970.

SDRs are a new form of money. Defined in terms of gold, with one unit equivalent to one US dollar they are held by central banks alongside gold, pounds and dollars. They differ from ordinary Drawing Rights in that only part of them is repayable. The rest in effect is a newly created asset.

SDRs are available to any IMF member participating in the Scheme, in relation to the quota of funds placed by him. Although allocated unconditionally, it is expected that SDRs be used only to alleviate balance of payment problems or to strengthen a country's reserves. In addition there is a stipulation that each participant country in a given distribution of SDRs has to accept additional SDRs to a total of twice the amount of its allocation, delivering convertible currencies against them in order to help finance the system. The reconstitution of SDRs is effected by the obligation of countries using them to reconstitute their position.

SDRs can be used in three ways:

1. as an addition to national gold and exchange reserves;
2. for the settlement of debts between central banks;
3. by central banks through the IMF, with the Fund designating a participant country to receive them in exchange for its currency.

Drawers are required to hold an average of 70% of the SDRs credited to them. If more than 30% of the SDRs are used the user has to buy them back, using other reserves in order to maintain his average. This means that, for every $10m SDRs allocated, $7m are a permanent addition to a country's reserves.

SDRs were conceived as a way of solving the deficits and surpluses of national balance of payments problems. Growth in the volume of world trade is facilitated by them because SDRs are created in accordance with international needs and in order to offset swings in balance of payment positions, and, for that matter, vagaries of the gold market. They are the first deliberate attempt to create a final reserve asset; that is to say, a reserve asset on par with and not convertible into gold. Restricted solely to international reserve purposes, SDRs bear no national mark - drawings being made against all member-currencies.

Before the introduction of SDRs all borrowings from the IMF were repayable. The IMF has always created international *liquidity* by swapping funds between member countries, but the issuing of SDRs to the IMF allowed it to create *new* money. Previously the only sources of international money alternative to gold were the British and US reserve currencies. SDRs thus orient the international monetary system more toward world-wide requirements.

Whether the SDRs do anything toward ending the massive flows of speculative capital that make world finance so unstable is another matter, however - one that depends on men developing a confidence in them equal to that inspired by gold.

# NOTES

# Full Title List

History of Money
*Gerard Klockenbring*

Prelude in Economics
*Christopher Houghton Budd*

Of Wheat and Gold
*Christopher Houghton Budd*

Beyond the Market
*Gaudenz Assenza*

Towards a New Economy
*Christopher Houghton Budd*

---

Economics
*Rudolf Steiner*

Rudolf Steiner's Social Intentions
*Rudi Lissau*

Threefold The Social Order
*Rudolf Steiner*

Rudolf Steiner, Economist
*Rudolf Steiner*

---

*Neweconomy* Magazine
Bimonthly Journal of Associative Economics

*For Information Contact:*
**New Economy Publications**
PO Box 341, Canterbury CT4 8GA, England